GuitarPlayer®

SESSIONS

Licks & Lessons
from the World's Greatest
Guitar Players
and Teachers

EDITED BY ANDY ELLIS

MF Miller Freeman Books

San Francisco

Published by Miller Freeman Books
600 Harrison Street, San Francisco, CA 94107
Publishers of *Keyboard, Bass Player,* and *Guitar Player*
magazines

un Miller Freeman
A United News & Media publication

Distributed to the book trade in the U.S. and Canada by
Publishers Group West, P.O. Box 8843, Emeryville, CA 94662

Distributed to the music trade in the U.S. and Canada by
Hal Leonard Publishing, P.O. Box 13819, Milwaukee, WI 53213

Design and Typesetting: Greene Design
Cover Design: Greene Design
Cover Photo: Peter Figen

Library of Congress Cataloging in Publication Data:

Guitar player sessions : licks & lessons from the world's great-
est guitar players and teachers / edited by Andy Ellis.
        p. cm.
Includes bibliographical references, discographies, and index.
ISBN 0-87930-503-7
1. Guitar—Studies and exercises.   I. Ellis, Andy, 1951– .
II. Guitar player
MT585.G956 1998
787.87'193X—dc21   98-30584
                                           CIP
                                           MN

Printed in the United States of America
98 99 00 01 02 03   5 4 3 2 1

TABLE OF CONTENTS

To hear the additional lessons from this book not found on the accompanying CD, you may contact NOTES ON CALL; for information see page 76.

INTRODUCTION

Looking for the next breakthrough? You'll find it in these pages—time and again. *Sessions* is a treasure chest of guitar techniques and musical ideas. It's packed with practical information—turnarounds, for instance, you can use on onstage tonight—as well as sophisticated concepts that will challenge your fingers and expand your mind.

Not another scale compilation or chord dictionary—there are already plenty of those—*Sessions* is a unique collection of lessons written by some of the finest pickers and teachers on the planet. These guitarists have distilled years of playing and studying into succinct, thought-provoking workouts, many of which are rendered on the companion CD. Use these audio examples to refine your phrasing and tone.

Guitar books written by one author offer a single point of view. By contrast, *Sessions* approaches the fretboard, harmony, improvisation, and music theory from dozens of angles, letting you forge your own understanding of our magnificent instrument. You'll benefit from the wisdom of such greats as George Van Eps, Steve Morse, the Edge, Ronnie Earl, Greg Martin, Lenny Breau, Steve Vai, David Grissom, Duke Robillard, Mike Stern, Bob Brozman, Barney Kessel, Ray Flacke, and Bugs Henderson. Featuring chords to stretch your ears, lines to spark your imagination, and studies to bust your chops, *Sessions* represents a balanced approach to learning guitar.

Best of all, you'll have fun—no need to start at page 1 and grind your way to the end, as with traditional method books. Instead, when you feel the urge to improve your playing, simply browse through this material and latch onto a lesson that inspires you. Let your intuition guide your eyes and hands.

Chosen for their content and inspiration, these lessons are drawn from the pages of *Guitar Player* magazine's "Sessions" section. If you enjoy freeform, non-linear learning, check out GP each month.

In the meantime, grab your tools—guitar, portable recorder, metronome, and a cup of java—and settle in for a great ride. Whether you love blues, rock, country, jazz, or folk, wield an electric or acoustic ax, or fingerpick or flatpick, *Sessions* has what you need to lift your playing to the next level.

— ANDY ELLIS

THE POWER OF 3 AND 7

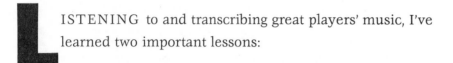

BY FRED HAMILTON

L ISTENING to and transcribing great players' music, I've learned two important lessons:

■ Within melodic lines and comping figures, the placement and resolution of the 3rd and 7th chord tones is crucial to establishing strong tonal centers.

■ Anticipated chord tones—those played on the upbeat before a chord—provide forward motion.

Listen to Art Blakey's *Mosaic*, John Coltrane's *Blue Train*, and Wayne Shorter's *Speak No Evil*. These and other great jazz recordings contain arrangements that demonstrate the power of the 3rd and 7th. The two- and three-horn harmonizations, backgrounds, and counterlines commonly use these chord tones with appropriate resolutions.

With a metronome set on two and four, play a bass line or the roots for the chord progression in Ex. 1 several times and tape it. Next play the notated 3rd and 7th parts over the rhythm track. Hear how these resolutions create a strong harmonic pull?

Create *rhythmic* pull by anticipating the resolutions. Play Ex. 2's two-horn backgrounds over your taped bass line. Finally, add a melodic line to fill in between the resolutions (Ex. 3).

Apply these concepts to tunes with IIm-V-I root motion. Study the masters: Jim Hall for economy and clarity, Jimmy Raney for articulations and bop lines, and Wes Montgomery for killer groove. Play with good time and have a good time!

Ex. 1

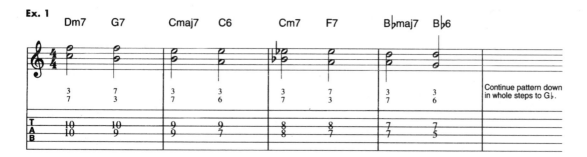

Ex. 2

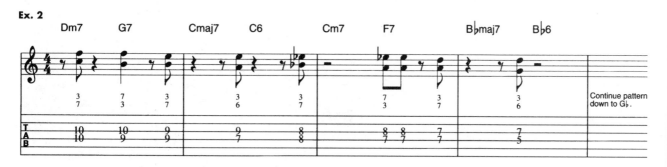

Ex. 3

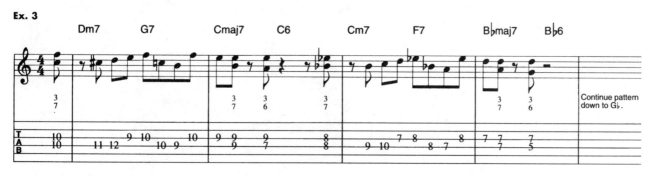

LAPTOP GUITAR PRIMER

BY DAVID HAMBURGER

PLAYING GUITAR "Hawaiian style"—resting it across your lap and applying a steel bar or slide from *above* the strings—opens up many possibilities beyond the realm of standard slide. If you don't have an old pawnshop lap steel lying neglected in the closet or a $4,000 Style 4 National Tricone squareneck hanging in your front hall, don't despair. Simply spring for a $5 nut adapter to raise the action on a normal 6-string. A thumbpick, two fingerpicks, and a Stevens steel—a solid, grooved slide favored by Dobro-ists—will complete your setup. Heavier strings, such as the commercially available "Dobro set" (.016-.059, low to high), will dramatically improve your tone, but check with a trusted repair person before restringing an instrument you care about, or the high action could become permanent in a couple of weeks.

Tune to the standard Dobro *G* tuning (*G, B, D, G, B, D,* low to high) and start with the old-time country phrases in Examples 1 and 2. Check out Clell "Cousin Jody" Sumney and Pete "Bashful Brother Oswald" Kirby on early Roy Acuff records to hear these licks in context. (While you're at it, give yourself a mysterious family nickname, like Dave "Mother-in-law Watson" Hamburger, for example.)

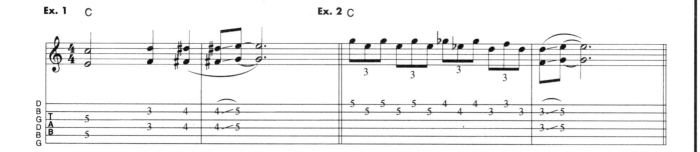

Buck "Uncle Josh" Graves almost single-handedly invented bluegrass Dobro in the 1950s, combining bluesy licks, a no-holds-barred attack, and plenty of open strings as he twisted boss Earl Scruggs' banjo rolls to nefarious purposes on a square-neck, wood-body Dobro. In Examples 3 and 4, drop the bar quickly and cleanly onto the strings just like you would for a guitar hammer-on.

Occasionally blues cats have played lap style, in contrast to the ever-present bottleneck stylists. Babe "Black Ace" Turner played solo on a National Tricone squareneck guitar, and Houston's Hop Wilson picked an electric lap steel with a full band in the early 1960s. Both of the licks in Examples 5 and 6 work in either context.

(continued on next page)

Western swing players such as Leon McAuliffe started out on acoustic flat-tops, adding pickups before moving on to 6- and 8-string and eventually double- and triple-neck electric steels with legs. Retune to *G6* (*G, B, D, E, G, B,* low to high—tune the top three strings *down*), and try the two 1940s-approved moves in Examples 7 and 8. On the former, mute with the left hand after the first three notes and again after the next three notes. Do this by lifting the bar from the strings while continuing to rest your left pinky on them.

Ex. 7 B♭6

Ex. 8 B♭6

DRONES
AND ECHOS

BY THE EDGE

I DON'T PLAY PROPER GUITAR. For a start, I avoid the major third like the plague. I like the ambiguity between major and minor chords, so I tread a very fine line between the two. I tend to shrink chords down to two or three notes plus octaves of those notes. For an *E* chord, I play just *B*s and *E*s, including my big *E* string. "Pride," for example, is really just a couple of strings. The critical thing is the echo. I'm playing sixteenth-notes, and the echo device supplies the triplet, so it's very fast.

I've experimented a lot with damping my guitar strings, using felt or gaffer's tape over the strings near the bridge to give zero sustain. Using echo, I've found some remarkable effects. The intro to "Wire" is a case in point: Having dampened the strings with tape and using a bottleneck and an echo setting, I got this incredible sound. It was quite Eastern, but really bizarre. Because I rarely rehearse, I haven't formed ruts down the fingerboard by playing the same things. It's still very unexplored territory.

A JAZZY TURNAROUND

BY BUGS HENDERSON

WHEN YOU PLAY a tune, it's tempting to color it with a lot of chords. But if you pack *too* many chords in there—especially during the verses—you can lose the song's feeling. It's often better to save the fancy fretwork for a turnaround.

A cool turnaround gives you a little break. For many guitarists, it's a chance to go, "Look what I can do. I may be playing rhythm, but when I get to this turnaround, I can play these cool chords."

For such occasions, here's a jazzy turnaround in the key of *F.* You can play it two ways: as a two-bar turnaround to a simple *Fmaj7* or as written, with bar 3's melodic flourish. The latter turns this turnaround into an ending.

Take a close look at the first two bars. All four chords have
a common tone in the top voice. Notice the descending
chromatic line on the second string that spans both measures.
The two chords in bar 1 share a common tone on the third
string (C♮), as do the two chords in bar 2 (B♭).

To control the relative volumes of each voice, play these
chords fingerstyle. After the pull-off in bar 3, let the open first
string ring out against the subsequent F major arpeggio. And
watch that slide: By sustaining beat three's E against the final F
triad, you create an *Fmaj7*.

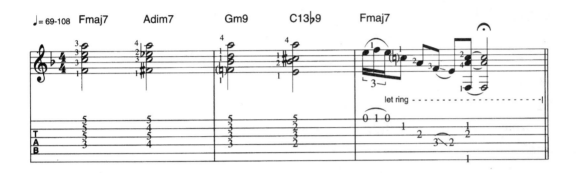

SUPER CHUCK

BY JIM CAMPILONGO

IT'S ALWAYS FUN to add a few twists to the classic Chuck Berry rhythm riff (Ex. 1), which you can play straight or with a swing feel. I discovered my first variation trying to decode Jerry Reed's "Tupelo Mississippi Flash." I never got that tune exactly right, but I've learned many good licks trying to assimilate something I couldn't quite hear. On a country gig, whenever the singer calls a number I've never heard, I smile and play Ex. 2. I inevitably get looks of admiration for "nailing" what was on the record.

Examples 3 and 4 are alternate blues-shuffle figures. The former is fairly simple and works well supporting vocals. The latter really swings and could push a soloist over the top.

CONTRARY BLUE

BY DREW BEARSE

HERE'S A TRICK for adding contrary motion into your blues licks," says Drew Bearse, a longtime *GP* reader who hails from Portland, Oregon. "This lick spans the critical V7-IV7-I7 transition of a 12-bar progression. The contrary motion occurs from the end of bar 1 into the beginning bar 2 (the *D9* to *C9* axis). Dig the two chromatic lines that move in opposition: *D-D♯-E* ascends, *C-B-B♭* descends. You're shrinking a minor seventh to a diminished fifth—the IV chord's tritone. It's a neat way to slip into the subdominant. Try this lick with a round, fruity Bluesbreakers tone and give the notes their full value."

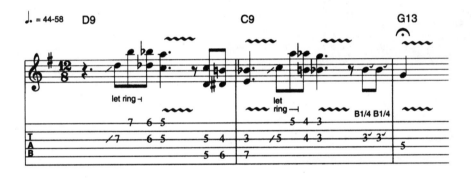

SWING COMPING

BY DUKE ROBILLARD

PHOTO: TRACY HART

WHEN COMPING in swing jazz and jump blues, I try to voice chords to create stepwise connecting lines within the harmony. I'm inspired by Count Basie's Kansas City sound and the great T-Bone Walker.

To get a feel for this horn-inspired harmony, listen carefully to the first three bars in Ex. 1, a 12-bar blues. Notice the top common tone and how the lowest two strings alternate between common tones and half-step movement. In bar 2, an ascending chromatic line on the second string ties the *Cm7, C#dim7,* and *Bb9* chords together. The overall result is dense, colorful harmony.

As you work through the progression, take time to track the melodic movement on each string. Listen for stepwise lines, such as in Ex. 2, the main internal melody for the first five bars.

Imagine each string is a horn; you forge progressions not by
linking a sequence of discrete fretboard grips, but by guiding
and blending three or four independent melodies from measure
to measure. It's an ear-expanding experience.

Ex. 1

Ex. 2

ELVIS EATS CHEESEBURGERS

BY GREG MARTIN

HERE'S A GREASY, quasi-steel-guitar lick that works well as either a country-fried blues or honky-tonk turnaround. The lick outlines *D*, *C*, *Bm*, *Am*, and *G*—a diatonic V-IV-IIIm-IIm-I progression in the key of *G*.

Some pointers: Use a flatpick on the third string and your middle finger on the first string. Watch the first release (bar 1, beat two); the trick is to stay in tune while easing the whole-step bend down to a half-step bend. In bar 2, keep the half-step slide smooth so it mimics the preceding release. Observe the *let ring* markings that define the lick's three phrases. Use a snappy tone and add reverb to taste. Viva Las Vegas!

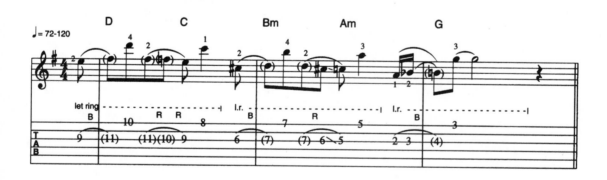

STEVE MORSE'S KEY TONE THEORY
AS TOLD TO GUITAR PLAYER

ANY PROGRESSION has key notes or tones that change with the harmony. A simple example is going from a rock and roll *C5*—a *C* power chord without the third—to an *A* major chord. Your first and only key tone change is from *C♮* to *C♯*. Almost any note you hit in a *C* scale, except for the *B♭* found in *C* blues or *C* Mixolydian, will work over *A*. Your main concern will be to change every *C♮* to *C♯*. This means you don't have to use any scales; simply play melodic lines in *C*, and then continue from right where you left off using the same notes you were playing. Just change *C♮* to *C♯* and avoid *B♭*.

Key tones in modes. To me, a mode is just a convenient way of describing a group of key tones. Once I understood what a Dorian mode was, I would never think of it as part of some other major scale. I'd think of it as a "minor/♭7t/♮ 6" scale. [The Dorian formula is 1, 2, ♭3, 4, 5, 6, ♭7.] That's it. Never another thought about it. I think of Mixolydian as a "major/♭7" scale. [The Mixolydian formula is 1, 2, 3, 4, 5, 6, ♭7.] I don't worry about which major scale a mode is related to. It's best to think of what a mode *sounds* like rather than what major scale it's derived from. Just focus on the special notes a mode contains: This is a dominant 7 with a G3 [Mixolydian] or ♮3 [Dorian], for example.

STORMIN' THE BLUES

BY DAVE RUBIN

I N THE '30s, Kansas City swing masters such as Count Basie and Jay McShann had blues in their souls and jazz harmony in their heads. Though they often played straight I-IV-V progressions, they reveled in arranging more sophisticated structures based on chord substitutions. Bessie Smith sang to these expanded harmonies in the '20s, but it took T-Bone Walker in the '40s to bring it on home to the blues community. In 1947 he waxed "Call It Stormy Monday," and *the* slow blues classic was born. Bobby Blue Bland's sublime 1961 cover, featuring Wayne Bennett's cool comping and lyrical solo, became the standard, the blueprint for the Allmans' version on *Live at Fillmore East* in 1971. Let's explore "Stormy Monday" and learn ways to jazz it up.

The tune operates marvelously at both slow and brisk bebop tempos. Take a gander at Ex. 1, bars 7-10, and you'll understand how the progression differs from your garden-variety 12-bar

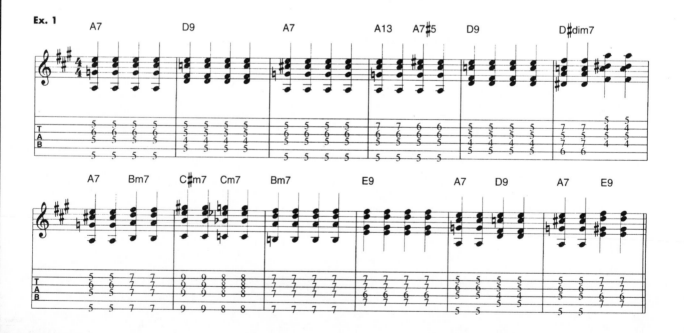

Ex. 1

blues. Instead of the typical two bars of I7, one bar of V7, and one bar of IV7, we have a diatonic pattern fleshed out with a chromatic passing chord: I-IIm-IIIm-♭IIIm-IIm-V7.

Slide *F#7#9*—the VI7—in place of the *Cm7* in bar 8 (Ex. 2) to create a four-bar backcycling pattern. Check out the fourths root motion: *C#-F#-B-E-A-D*.

The Allmans subbed a melodious *B♭maj7* for *E9* (the V7) in bar 10. Ex. 3 shows the recommended voicing. It links *Bm7* to *A7* with two descending chromatic lines: *F#-F♮-E* on the top, *B-B♭-A* on the bottom. Spot the two common tones between *Bm7* and *B♭maj7*?

Ex. 2

Ex. 3

Ex. 4 drops into bars 10, 11, and 12. Bar 10 features *E7#9*'s tritone twin, *B♭13* (see page 33). Diminished passing chords spice up bars 11 and 12.

You'll swear your svelte solidbody has mutated into a big ol' archtop when you play Ex. 5. Replace bars 7-10 with this chromatic honey. That last *B♭9* is a tritone sub for *E9*. Yeah, we're stompin' at the Savoy now!

(continued on next page)

Ex. 4

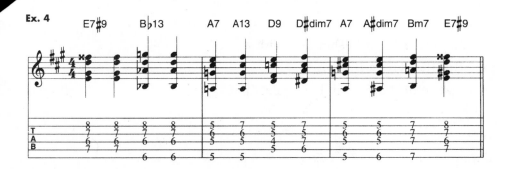

Ex. 5

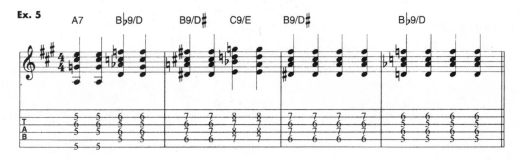

GEORGE VAN EPS ON CHORDS AND SWIMMING LESSONS
AS TOLD TO GUITAR PLAYER

CHORD NAMES ARE in my subconscious, and I'm aware of them. But I'm more conscious of them as a collection of lines that swim—they're going someplace. If the lines are swimming, let them go where they want, because they are free entities. And if they wind up in utter disaster, don't give up; give them swimming lessons. If I start to think, "This is this chord, and that is that chord, and when this note changes while that line moves against these sustained notes it becomes this chord," it's too academic. It's no longer music in my mind; I'm making a calculator out of it. I want to listen to those tones, to the overall effect. If I don't, I won't be able to guide those lines that want to go someplace. It's all about intervals—that's the way my mind works—and they don't have to have any names. They are just this far apart or that far apart. I'm conscious of each note's relationship to every other note; it's actually an air gap.

ROCKABILLY STRETCHES OF DOOM

BY JOE DALTON

YOU CAN COP the sound of a swing-band horn section with close-voiced chords. Such harmony works particularly well in rockabilly, which often features smooth, gliding chords or biting stabs for a souped-up big band sound.

On guitar, close voicings require wide stretches. Limber up with Ex. 1. Let each string sustain and strive for a clean, articulated sound. With daily practice, you'll be able to play this exercise even on the challenging lower frets.

Ex. 2 shows close-voiced *E6*, *A9*, and *B7* chords (the I, IV, and V of *E*), each with three useful inversions. Familiarize yourself with these finger-stretchers, and then work out common changes, such as I-IV-V-I (Ex. 3a), V-I (Ex. 3b), and I-IV-I (Ex. 3c).

Pay attention to harmonic details—they'll help you memorize these new formations. For example, notice how the *E6* to *A9* change in Ex. 3a results from moving *G♯* to *G♮*. Such subtle voice-leading creates smooth chord-to-chord transitions.

Don't settle for one way to play a change—keep digging for other useful fingerings (Ex. 4). Mix 'em up: Try changing chords across string sets. For instance, can you find the twelfth-position *E6-B7* move that jumps the same formation from the top four strings to the middle four?

Once you've got a grip on the 12-bar changes in *E*, transpose them, gradually moving down the fretboard to increase the burn. These smooth-sounding stretches merit many hours of experimenting, listening, and playing, and will freshen your rockabilly, R&B, country, and swing rhythm parts.

Ex. 1

etc.

Ex. 2

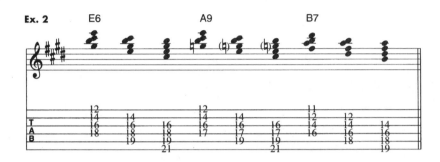

Ex. 3a **Ex. 3b** **Ex. 3c**

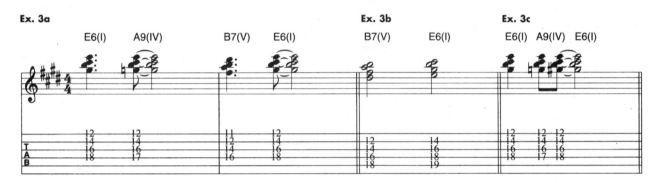

Ex. 4

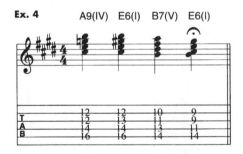

HEAD-TURNING CASCADES

BY STEVE TROVATO

MIXING OPEN STRINGS with fretted notes lets you produce unusual interval skips and cascading, harp-like runs. It's similar to playing piano while holding down the sustain pedal. Though associated with country, this technique works in any style.

Let's explore ways to create this ringing sound. First, a few practice tips:

- Use a clean tone with lots of treble and a little reverb.
- To enhance the shimmer, add a bit of chorus.
- Arch your fingers, keeping them perpendicular to the fingerboard so the strings can ring against each other.
- Use a hybrid right-hand technique, alternating between pick and middle finger (*m*).
- Pluck all open strings with *m*.
- Equalize pick and finger attack to maintain even dynamics. (Try growing your right-hand nails approximately ⅛" and coating them with clear nail polish.)
- Angle your picking wrist slightly downward so your fingers pull straight up on the strings.

Ex. 1 uses a *G* major pentatonic scale and sounds great as a country tag or ending. This lick works over *G* or *Em*. Try it each way and note the difference. Begin picking with your middle finger and maintain an alternating finger/pick pattern, except for notes 4 and 5, which are both plucked with *m*.

Ex. 2 is a IIm-V7-I in *C* played over *Dm*, *G7*, and *C*. Again, start with *m* and alternate with the flatpick. Watch the hammers. In bar 4, beat two, use your ring finger (*a*) to pluck high *B*. Pop that last pedal-steel bend with pick, *m*, and *a*.

Ex. 3, which comes courtesy of fusion great Don Mock, outlines an *E7#9* chord. The lick works against a static *E7* chord, as

well as over an *E7* to *A* (or *Am*) change. This time, start with
the pick and alternate with *m*.

I discovered Ex. 4's *B* harmonic minor run by accident one
day when I fumbled Ex. 1. Use alternate hybrid picking, leading
with *m*. Pluck notes 4 and 5.

This cascade technique offers a wealth of possibilities.
Experiment and have fun.

THRASH AND GRIND PATTERNS

BY MIKE HICKEY

GRAB A BARITONE electric (tuned *B, E, A, D, F#, B*—see page 54 for details), dial up some distortion, and try these rhythm patterns on the open sixth string. Ex. 1a, with its downstroke eighth-notes, recalls Judas Priest. Watch the picking indications in Examples 1b, 1c, and 1d.

Add Ex. 2's power chords and diads to the low-string rhythms. Each interval's root is circled; use your ear to discover cool progressions. Mute and chunk!

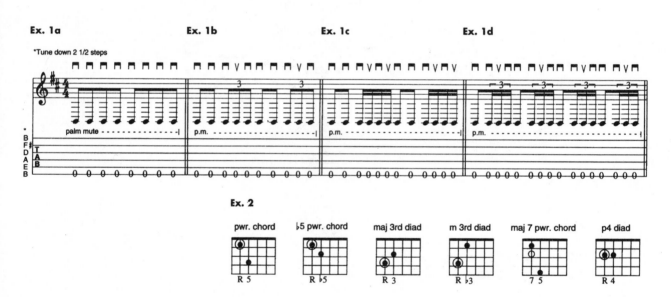

RALPH TOWNER ON FINGERSTYLE 12-STRING
AS TOLD TO GUITAR PLAYER

FINGERPICKING a 12-string can be problematic. If you lift *up* on a string, you'll lose all your sound; it'll evaporate. Lifting up can cause you to miss the second string and break your fingernails. Here's how to hear both strings simultaneously and spare your nails: The double strings form a little plateau, a plane. Push *down* on those two strings as if they were a wide band. Develop a push-and-roll technique. Pluck on a very flat plane—make the strings vibrate horizontally, parallel to the guitar top—to bring out the sound.

COMPING THE BLUES

BY LENNY BREAU

JAZZ PLAYERS OFTEN embellish standard 12-bar, I-IV-V blues progressions with substitute and passing chords, extra IIm-V-I cadences, and backcycling progressions. You have to hear these changes before you can start intelligently applying them to your music, and that means learning some jazzed-up blues progressions.

Four-to-the-bar comping is a good place to start. The late Freddie Green, Count Basie's longtime guitarist, was the acknowledged master of this style. He typically used three-note chords voiced on the sixth, fourth, and third strings. These chords sound full and work well for straight rhythm, despite their abbreviated size.

Using a flatpick, play the following *C* blues progression with crisp, ringing downstrokes. Carefully mute the first, second, and fifth strings. Tape the changes and improvise over them using a *C* blues scale. You'll find that familiar blues licks suddenly sound fresh and jazzy against more complex changes.

Some quick observations:

■ In bars 2 and 6, the *F♯dim7* passing chord moves you smoothly from *F* (or *F7*), the IV, back to *C* (or *C6*), the I.

■ If you view bar 5's *F7* as a temporary I, the preceding *Gm7-C7* change becomes a IIm-V ramp into *F7*.

■ Two more IIm-V-I cadences occur in bars 8 through 11 (*Em7-A7-D7* and *Dm7-G7-C7*). The last three dominant 7s backcycle in fourths to the tonic: *A7-D7-G7-C6*. With their strong resolution, the IIm-V-I changes and backcycling dominants provide forward motion, pulling you through the progression and ultimately back to the top.

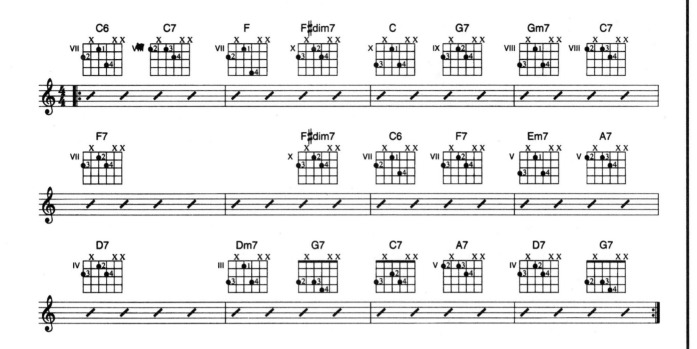

BRAZILIAN FINGERSTYLE PATTERNS

BY TIM SPARKS

BRAZIL'S MUSIC IS one of the happier products of the marriage of African, European, and Native American cultures in the Western hemisphere. Brazilian-style guitar percolates with rhythms that derive in part from religious traditions that slaves brought to the New World. In the belief system known as *Candomble*, African deities are associated with specific rhythms and tonalities. In the practice of *Batuque* and *Umbanda*, music is a bridge to the spirit world. What might seem a raucous percussion ensemble is, on a deeper level, an invocation that gives Brazil's popular music a deep spiritual subtext.

The following examples come from Nilton Rangel, who teaches and performs with the Orchestra de Pernambuco in Recife, Brazil. Their basic comping patterns are derived from the *batucada*, a percussion ensemble that figures in recreational and religious celebrations. The thumb mimics the rhythm of the *surdo*, a large bass drum. Against the thumb, the fingers pick out syncopated patterns corresponding to the *tamborim*, a small, hand-held frame drum that leads the batucada.

The most important point for beginning in Brazilian-style guitar is this: The thumb plays on the beat and the fingers syncopate. If necessary, you can start with the picking hand alone, using open or muted strings. When the left and right hands feel comfortable and it sounds good, you can add some fancier bass lines.

Ex. 1 is part of a family of percussive motifs known as *maracatu*. Centered in Recife, this tradition has endured since slave times. During Carnaval, thousands of drummers congregate in downtown Recife to celebrate the anointing of a king for the African community.

Ex. 1

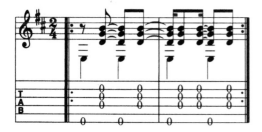

Examples 2 and 3 are built on the architecture of Ex. 1 and reflect the style of Joao Gilberto, Baden Powell, and others who incorporated syncopated elements into the bossa nova beginning in the late 1950s. Bossa nova, roughly translated as "new wave," was a cool refinement of the exuberant samba. Solo guitar was well suited to the sensibility of the urban poets, drawing inspiration from the Africanized street slang of Brazilian Portuguese. North Americans were introduced to the bossa nova primarily through the work of Sergio Mendes, Charlie Byrd, and Astrud Gilberto, who had a huge success with "Girl from Ipanema." With songs by Tom Jobim and Luiz Bonfa, the movie *Black Orpheus* also brought the music to U.S. audiences.

Ex. 2

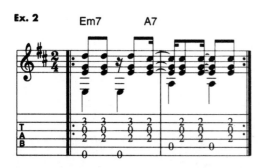

Ex. 3

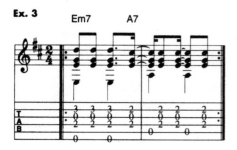

(continued on next page)

The central character in *Black Orpheus* is a guitarist who journeys to the underworld and duels with death in an effort to save his girlfriend.

Ex. 4 recalls the style of Gilberto Gil. The muted percussive notes are created by immediately lifting the fret hand to dampen the sound while still touching the strings. Gilberto Gil, along with Milton Nascimento, Caetano Veloso, Chico Buarque, and Joao Bosco, to name a few, reinvented the bossa nova, and the new sound became known as *tropicalismo*. Tropicalismo goes back to deep African roots in Bahia as well as Caribbean styles such as reggae. David Byrne has documented this movement by assembling an excellent series of compilation discs for Sire/Warner Bros.

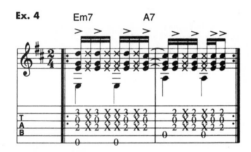

STEVE KHAN ON TRANSCRIBING AND IMPROVISING
AS TOLD TO GUITAR PLAYER

TRANSCRIBING IS AN introverted, lonely pursuit. Sometimes you don't think anyone else in the world is doing it until you get together with other musicians and realize it's a fairly universal activity. For instance, sax players transcribe John Coltrane, Lester Young, Wayne Shorter, and Charlie Parker. Transcribing and analyzing solos is great as long as you don't forget the artist was *improvising*, and not thinking things out. As you get familiar with a player's style, you start making connections, such as noticing the same rhythmic phrase but with different notes.

Misconceptions about improvising put pressure on less-experienced players. The idea that you shouldn't repeat yourself is a jazz myth. Basically, you have a vocabulary you draw from. In an improvisation, you may play something you've never played before. That's a great feeling. If I come away from an evening having experienced a couple of exhilarating moments, I feel good.

THE HICCUP METHOD

BY CHARLES H. CHAPMAN

HERE'S A QUICK AND DIRTY way to play bass lines and chords simultaneously. Though this "hiccup" method is limited, it sounds funky, builds chops, and is a great way to get a bass-plus-chord technique up and running.

Play the following progression with a swing feel. Pluck the chords using index, middle, and ring fingers on the *D*, *G*, and *B* strings; hit the bass notes on the *A* and *E* strings with your thumb. The result: staggered chords, with their root on the downbeat and harmony on the upbeat. The walking bass line lets you groove without cluttering up the sound with too many chords.

Experiment with progressions of your own. Use common chord voicings that fall naturally on *D*, *G*, and *B* strings, and insert passing tones to smooth out the bass lines. As you change chords, try to move each note by only a whole- or half-step. Above all, trust your ear, and you'll groove with the best.

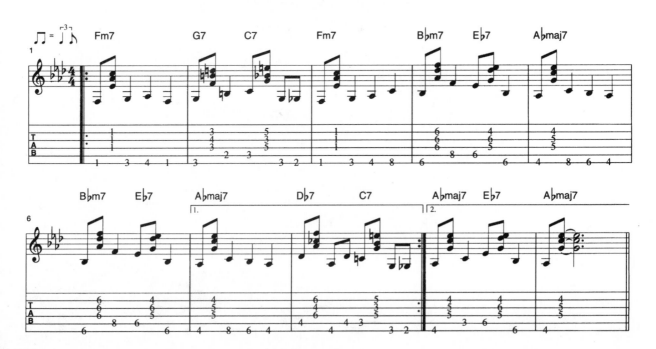

TRITONE TWINS AND THE FLAT-FIVE SUBSTITUTION

BY ANDY ELLIS

THE TRITONE—an interval of three whole-steps or a diminished fifth—divides an octave in half. Inverted, this symmetrical interval remains a tritone. In a dominant 7th chord, the 3rd and ♭7th degrees form a tritone. For example, *E7*'s tritone is *G♯-D*. Invert this, and you get *D-G♯* (*A♭*), the 3rd and ♭7th of *B♭7*. Since *E7* and *B♭7* are tritone twins, you can substitute one for the other. You can swap any two dominants (i.e., dominant 7th, 9th, or 13th chords) whose roots are a diminished fifth apart. This "flat-five substitution" is a jazz mainstay.

MIKE STERN'S SINGLE-STRING ARPEGGIOS
AS TOLD TO GUITAR PLAYER

PIANIST CHARLIE BANACOS is an amazing teacher who helped me a lot. He taught me single-string exercises that involve playing arpeggios on each string, all the way up and down the fingerboard. He figures many guitarists already know how to play in position. He observed that Wes Montgomery played up and down. Pat Metheny and Mick Goodrick also stress playing along the fingerboard.

For example, take a *Cmaj7* arpeggio with added ♯11, 9, and 13. On the low-E string, play *C* at the 8th fret, *E* at the 12th fret, *G* at the 15th fret, *B* at the 19th fret, and then come back down (Ex. 1). So that you cover the entire string, play an open *E—C* major's 3— then *G* at the 3rd fret, *B* at the 7th fret—now you're using the added notes—*D* at the 10th fret, *F*♯ at the 14th fret, and *A* at the 17th fret (Ex. 2). Don't forget to descend.

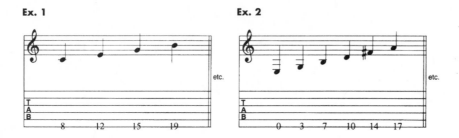

Ex. 1   Ex. 2

Fingering doesn't matter. This isn't about technique; it has more to do with playing slowly and listening. Once you finish the arpeggio on one string, transfer it to the others. Play the arpeggio in as many places on each string as possible.

Then there are a whole slew of related exercises. For instance, you can embellish each chord tone by approaching from
a half-step below (Ex. 3) or from a scale step above (Ex. 4). Next
you can put the two together, playing a scale step above the
chord tone, a half-step below, then the chord tone itself (Ex. 5).

Practice these ideas on each string and in all keys. Eventually you'll find yourself developing more freedom in playing
single-note lines.

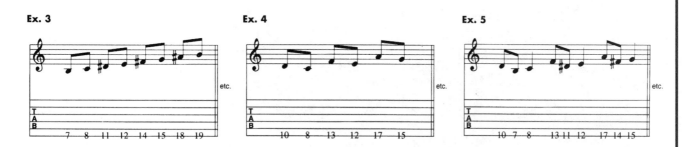

Ex. 3 **Ex. 4** **Ex. 5**

STRETCHING THE LIVE WIRE

BY KEITH WYATT

WITHOUT SACRIFICING NUANCE, the late Albert King forged a raw, powerful blues style that featured an intense attack, aggressive phrasing, and enormous bends. Albert's unique tuning and the way he held his ax (he was a lefty playing a flipped-over guitar with the low strings closest to his shoes) were a big part of his sound, as was his use of bare fingers for picking.

We can all draw inspiration from Albert's outrageous string bending. Here's a King-influenced solo for a slow 12-bar shuffle in *A*. It's in the tenth position, mostly on the second string. You can also try it on the first string, fifth position. Bending here is more difficult—we're talking two whole-steps—but the tone is noticeably clearer, and the challenge of reaching the highest notes will definitely add intensity.

The solo's main technical requirements are strength and accuracy. Use your 3rd finger for all the bends, supported by the first two for added strength. Carefully bend to pitch, striving to match the equivalent fretted notes. Once you can consistently bend in tune—no mean feat—start listening for notes *between* the frets. These tones lie where slide players dwell. You won't find this zone on a fret or a keyboard. It's an essential part of the deep blues sound. Listen to Albert's solo on "Personal Manager" to hear how deliberately shading a note slightly sharp or flat can give it special character.

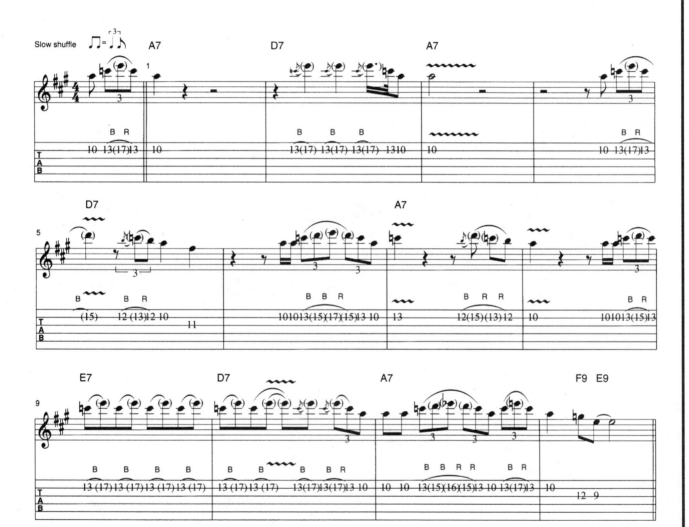

THE SPIDER CRAWL

BY ANDY ELLIS

HERE'S A KNUCKLE-BUSTER I learned from John Knowles, ace Nashville fingerpicker and Chet Atkins cohort. Start off slowly, using a metronome to keep solid time, and work your way up and down the neck. Be sure your paired fingers (1st/3rd, 2nd/4th) land simultaneously—don't let them flam. Lift your 1st and 3rd fingers the instant your 2nd and 4th fingers fret the strings and vice versa. (Imagine your digits are little pistons firing two at a time in perfect sync.) Play legato, using crisp downstrokes.

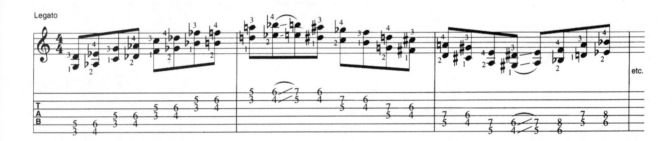

DAVID LINDLEY'S CREATIVE AMNESIA
AS TOLD TO GUITAR PLAYER

I HAVE A FUNNY kind of concentration when I play. You're conscious of the band, but the band is so locked in, it eliminates the fighting-for-time element. So that's secure, and you can take that for granted—put it up in the left-hand corner. So you're playing the guitar, and you're standing there—I'm just thinking of the best times, and there are very few where it really happens—and you're not inside yourself, and you're not in the guitar. You're about three feet in front of yourself. That's what it feels like. It's one of those things people will be trying to explain forever and ever.

The rest of the time, which is about 90 percent of the time, you're just listening to yourself, and you get sidetracked. Things come into your mind, like, "Uh-oh, I have to sing another verse." That's where the practice and rehearsal pays off. You get everything second-nature and go out and play, and you can stop thinking. But that takes an incredible amount of discipline.

On the spur of the moment you can have tiny flashes, like, "Hey, why don't you mess around with octaves here?" or "Let's play this like a horn." But it's like driving a car. You don't stop and think, "Now I will move this foot and go 50 miles an hour instead of 44." It just comes out. It's like arriving at your destination without remembering making any of the turns. Sleeping through West Covina. That's exactly what it is.

PHOTO: RANDEE ST. NICHOLAS

COLOSSAL VOICINGS

BY JOHN STOWELL

CHORDS BUILT BY stacking very close or large intervals make intriguing alternatives to standard forms voiced in thirds. You can reinvigorate tired progressions by weaving new harmonic color into them. It's a simple, three-step process:

■ Analyze a chord's formula and interval makeup.

- Locate available notes that can enrich the harmony.

- Integrate these new notes into the chord, looking for opportunities to replace thirds with seconds, sixths, sevenths— even ninths.

For example, *Cmaj7* consists of the 1st, 3rd, 5th, and 7th degrees of a *C* major scale—*C, E, G, B*, or major third/minor third/major third. Incorporating other tones in the chord, such as *D* (the 9), *A* (6), *Gb* (lowered 5 or raised 11) and *G#* (raised 5), individually or in combination, expands your harmonic palette. Approach the process with an open mind, and the resulting voicings will expand your ears *and* fingers.

Let's explore the idea in the context of the classic IIm-V-I cadence (Examples 1 through 6). Don't be intimidated by these stretches. My hands aren't large, but because I like these sounds, I gradually developed a method using the *sides* as well as the tips of my fingers to accommodate some difficult inversions. Low action and light strings are helpful; I use an active Bartolini humbucker with the mids tuned up about 3/4 on my amp, and the sound is plenty fat. Some practice tips:

- If at first a fingering seems infeasible, just play a portion of the chord or take two or three notes from the new inversion and combine them with a chord you know.

- Determine where each embellishment is located. When, say, *Cmaj9* is indicated, find the *D*.

- Create new IIm-V-I progressions by mixing voicings from these six cadences.

- Where practical, use open strings to create otherwise impossible voicings.

Though the process begins with awkward new fingerings, it eventually becomes intuitive. Remember, nobody begins with smart ears or fingers. You'll gradually acquire great shapes and colors for comping and writing and develop an affinity for stretches. Supercharge your solos by extracting close-interval ideas from the chords. Be patient: There's still lots of unexplored territory on the fretboard.

(continued on next page)

Ex. 1

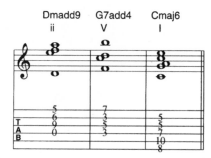

Ex. 2

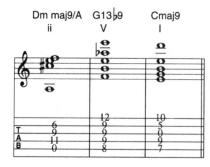

Ex. 3

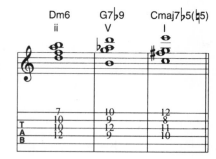

Ex. 4

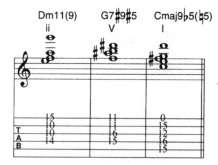

Ex. 5

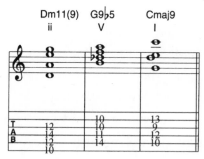

Ex. 6

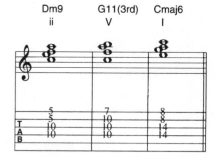

MICK GOODRICK
ON TEACHING
AS TOLD TO GUITAR PLAYER

THOSE WHO'VE STUDIED with Boston's guitar guru agree: Goodrick has a special gift for using similes and parables to inspire study and stimulate creative thought. In the following Zen-like musing, he sheds new light on the process of sharing musical knowledge.

I learn a lot from my students. Many people have the attitude that knowledge is a thing, like a hamburger. If I have a hamburger, and you're hungry, then I have to decide whether I want to give you some, which means there won't be as much for me. But information isn't like that. If I tell you something you don't know, I still have it. In addition, now that you have the information, I can get your reaction to it and see what you do with it that might be different. So I end up with more.

There's a story I like to tell about a man who falls into a deep hole. A couple of days later, he hears footsteps and yells for help, saying he'll do anything to get out. A boy leans over and says he'll pull the man up, but only if he promises to rescue ten other people from the same predicament. Teaching is a lot like that.

PHOTO: PAUL ROBICHEAU

WHAMMY-STEEL WORKOUT

BY MICHAEL LEE FIRKINS

CHET ATKINS WAS one of the first to use a vibrato bar to imitate a whining pedal steel. Listen to his 1952 recording of "Chinatown, My Chinatown" and smile. Although there's nothing like the real thing, you can lend a steel-like cry to your 6-string with subtle whammy moves.

The following example uses painful chord voicings and delicate vibrato-arm effects to imitate a Hawaiian guitar. Use your right thumb, index, and middle fingers to pluck each group of notes while your pinky manipulates the vibrato arm. Pay close attention to each group of grace notes. With the vibrato, lower each indicated chord a half-step. (Note: Due to differences in gauge and tension, the strings won't detune uniformly. That's okay. Use the highest string as your pitch guide.) Pluck and release slowly to standard pitch, being careful not to up-trem. In beats two and four of each bar, follow this vibrato maneuver by lowering the arm one half-step and then releasing it silently before plucking again.

Try a clean, warm tone with a touch of reverb—listen to Jimi's "The Wind Cries Mary." If the *C6* stretch gives you problems, clamp a capo on the 5th fret and play the whole passage up a fourth to ease the pain!

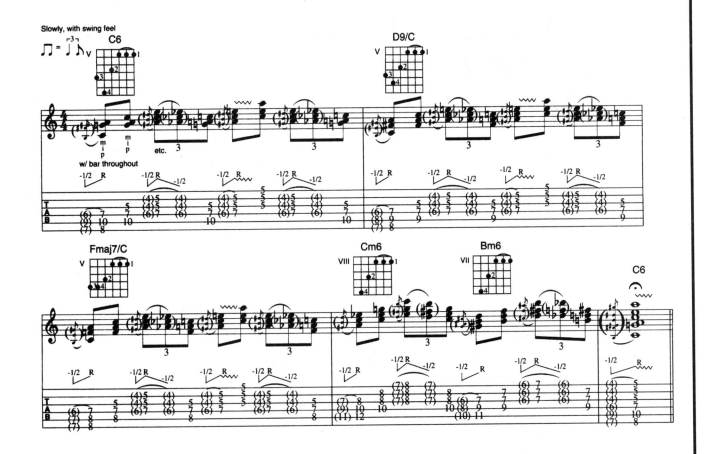

PAT MARTINO'S 12-POINT STAR
AS TOLD TO GUITAR PLAYER

How do you find fresh musical ideas?

I have a system of equations that immediately gives every chord on the guitar. They deal with ideas like rotation, which is a great way to overcome musical repetition. Take a chromatic scale from *C* to *C*, a 12-note sequence, and write it on the staff. Directly below that divide it into a six-note sequence, which will give you whole tones. Below that pull out the minor thirds of the four-note diminished sequence. Next write down the major thirds, a three-note sequence, and finally the tritone, or flatted fifth, which divides the 12-note sequence in half. Connect the *C* and *F♯* notes; you'll arrive at a 12-point star that shows a *balance* that permeates music itself. It's analogous to one point of music leading to another to create an idea, or in this case a picture. This is what I'm interested in and what I base my studies and analyses on.

The diagram's lines intersect a diminished 7th chord formed by the middle staff's minor thirds. What gives?

There are only four positions on the guitar before you have note duplication. The diminished chord shows you that: You have four diminished chords going up the fingerboard before you hit the fifth, which is a duplication. That's because the diminished chord is the division of one octave into four equal parts.

You don't use key signatures.

I don't relate to them. I see everything harmonically and in a more 12-tone sense. Chromaticism plays a heavy role in my music. You have to free yourself from locked-in and false perspectives, and use your imagination to create your own breathing on your instrument. This is where your creativity abides. When you create an idea, however, you must also create an audience. Nothing is totally new; only what is forgotten seems new.

PRE-BEND TWANGIN'

BY RAY FLACKE

THIS PASSAGE FEATURES tricky pedal-steel pre-bends. They're easy on a steel—you simply hit a pedal or knee lever before picking and releasing the notes. On the guitar, however, it's a manual process. Using your sense of touch, you have to bend silently into the note. Nailing the starting pitch—which requires a whole-step pre-bend—takes practice. Your best bet is to use a non-trem guitar with light strings. Try a hybrid picking grip: pick, middle, and ring fingers on the sixth, fifth, and third strings, respectively.

The low *E* sustains, creating a piano-like pedal tone beneath the moving harmony. Watch the fret-hand fingering. For added strength, bend with your 2nd finger supported by your 1st. Bar 3 contains a succession of whole- and half-step bends and releases. Beat four's hammer and pull provides a brief respite before the final pre-bend. If it hurts, just remember: Stretching's good for you.

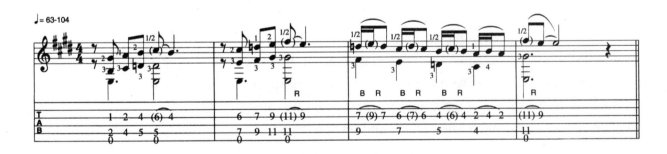

COUNTRY BLUES TURNAROUNDS

BY RONNIE EARL

HERE'S ONE OF MY favorite turnarounds. It's simple, versatile, and lends itself to cool variations. Let's first try it in *A* (Ex. 1). Mute the *G* string with either your 2nd or 1st finger—whichever is fretting the *D* string on a given beat. (Refer to indicated fingerings.) Use a pick/middle attack for the descending double-stops and your ring finger to pluck the high-*A* drone. The most important thing is to play with feeling.

This turnaround suggests melodic variations, as shown in Ex. 2. You can flatpick Ex. 2a, but in Ex. 2b squeeze the first triplet-eighth of each beat with pick and ring finger. The middle finger takes the second string all the way.

To get the most mileage out of this lick, relocate it on different string sets and then transpose it. As you move up and down the neck, pay attention to the top note, which is the root. In Ex. 3—we're still in *A*—drop the turnaround onto the second, third, and fifth strings. Though the fingering changes, the notes remain the same. After you've dug the new syncopated rhythm, try this fingering with the three triplet patterns from the previous examples. Finally, move the turnaround one string set lower to *E* (Ex. 4) for yet another fingering. The top common tone is still the root.

Ex. 1

(a)   **(b)**

Ex. 2

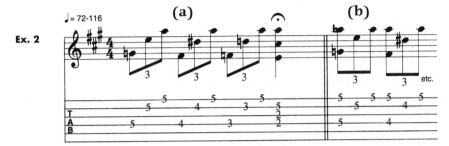

Ex. 3

Ex. 4

DOIN' THAT CRAZY HAND JIVE

BY BOB BROZMAN

TO SWING, you must feel two against three. You can accomplish this by learning to drum Ex. 1 with your bare hands. Internalizing this lopsided train rhythm will immensely improve your jazz comping, Delta blues finger-picking, and funk grooves. You'll play looser, yet with more control. Like ear training, rhythm training builds musicianship.

Playing two against three is pretty easy, once you grasp the pattern. The common denominator of two and three is six. Within a six-beat cycle, you thwack two beats with one hand, three with the other (Ex. 2). Notice how:

- The "two" hand plays on beats one and four.

- The "three" hand plays on beats one, three, and five.

- Both hands play one; beats two and six are silent.

To really *hear* what's happening, try drumming the rhythm on two different surfaces, say a table and your knee. Start slowly and count aloud (this is important). If it's not happening, switch hands. Eventually, as you tune into the rhythm, you can stop counting and just play the beat. Once you hear it, speed up. Finally, reverse hands and start all over again.

Ex. 1

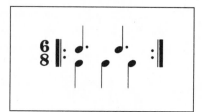

Ex. 2

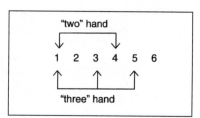

JOHN SCOFIELD'S POWER PENTATONICS
AS TOLD TO GUITAR PLAYER

YOU CAN USE pentatonics in many ways. In *G* minor, for example, try G minor, *D* minor, *C* dominant, *F* major, or *C* major pentatonic scales. As chords progress, an experienced musician may play notes from the previous pentatonic scale, altering only one note to fit the new harmony. For instance, play a *C* major pentatonic for *C*, and if the progression goes to *A7*, raise the *C* to *C♯*. That's showing real mastery over chords.

Here's what you need to know to explore these recipes:

- The minor pentatonic formula is 1, ♭3, 4, 5, ♭7. *G* minor and *D* minor pentatonic contain *G, B♭, C, D, F* and *D, F, G, A, C*, respectively.

- The dominant pentatonic formula is 1, 2, 3, 5, ♭7. *C* dominant pentatonic yields *C, D, E, G, B♭*.

- The major pentatonic formula is 1, 2, 3, 5, 6. *F* major and *C* major pentatonic comprise *F, G, A, C, D* and *C, D, E, G, A*.

STRING SKIPPING DELUXE

BY FRANK GAMBALE

SKIPPING STRINGS MAKES serious demands on your flatpicking technique. Here are some exercises designed to tackle typical picking problem areas. These examples start easy and get progressively harder. Play them at medium tempos. Accuracy is more important than speed; speed develops from accuracy.

Use alternate picking in Ex. 1, starting with an upstroke. Once you've nailed it, reverse the pattern and start with a downstroke. Ex. 2 alternates between two notes per string and skips, forcing you to switch between small and large right-hand moves. Ex. 3 features dispersed major triads; apply this concept to minor, augmented, and diminished triads as well. In Ex. 4, one- and two-string skips mix with adjacent-string picking. Notice how the alternate picking pattern flip-flops: Bar 1 starts with an upstroke, bar 2 with a downstroke. When skipping the melodic sixths in Ex. 5, use strict alternate picking.

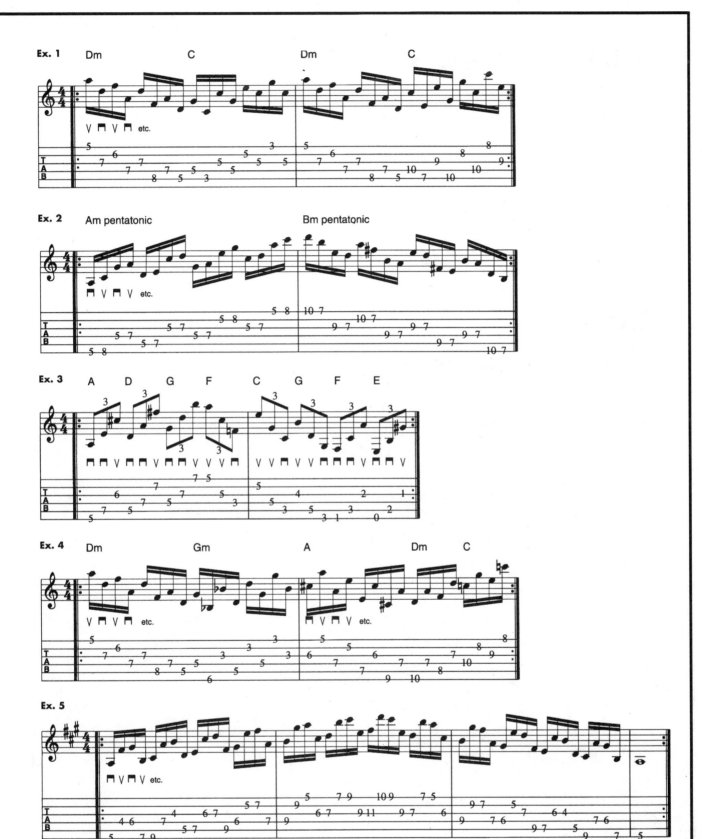

BARITONE GUITAR TIPS

BY ANDY ELLIS

string	6	5	4	3	2	1
pitch	B	E	A	D	F#	B
gauge	.065W	.052W	.042W	.032W	.018P	.014P

YOU CAN OFTEN convert a standard electric into a mighty baritone—or *B*-guitar—for subterranean twanging or thrashing (see Mike Hickey's "Thrash and Grind Patterns," p. 24). Start with the suggested string gauges shown here. For the bottom *B*, try a bass string. The lower four strings are wound; only the top two are plain. You'll likely have to widen the guitar's nut slots, and you'll need to adjust the intonation. On some guitars, the sixth string may be too stout to thread into its tuner post. If so, remove the tuner and have a machine shop drill out the hole. (The stock tuners on the Fender Standard American Strat work fine, and its nut is easy to widen or replace. You might consider converting this ax to a baritone.)

STRING
ENGLISH

BY B.B. KING

PHOTO: RANDI ANGLIN

Photo 1

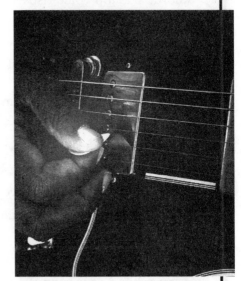

Photo 2   PHOTOS: JON SIEVERT

I PLAY MOSTLY downstrokes—which is why I'm not very fast—with a medium pick. I *hold* it with my thumb and index finger, and *control* it with my middle finger. I attack the strings harder than most people. At times I fight the strings for presence, to get that force.

Most of the time I don't hold the pick completely flat against the strings. I turn it so that it has a bit of an angle (Photo 1). When I want to mellow out, I hold the pick this way and get midway between the end of the neck and the bridge. But when I want a real staccato sound, I play near the bridge and hold the pick flat (Photo 2).

I take the extra effort to make sure I'm hitting the string where and how I want to hit it. It's almost like playing pool: You're going to use a certain bit of English.

MO' MIGHTY TURNAROUNDS

BY RONNIE EARL, GREG MARTIN & BUGS HENDERSON

HAUL OUT THE FINGEREASE: *Our turnaround trio is back, bearing cool new offerings you can use on the gig tonight. (See page 70 for another set of hip turnarounds from these three players.)* —AE

(See page 70 for another set of hip turnarounds from these three players.)

Ronnie Earl: "I like to play this jazzy turnaround in a slow blues or easy shuffle. It works well in all keys." Ex. 1 shows the passage in *A*. Drop the *C#m7-C9-Bm7-Bb7#9* change into the last two bars of a 12-bar blues. Notice how the diatonic *C#m7* and *Bm7* are each followed by passing chords (*C9* and *Bb7#9*). Though they're a half-step lower, the passing chords retain a common tone with their respective diatonic buddies. Dig the slick contrary motion as you move from diatonic to passing chord: The top voice rises stepwise while the remaining two notes drop a half-step. Be sure to emphasize *B-Bb-A-Ab-G*, the fourth-string descending chromatic line that drives the progression home to *A13* and brings you to the start of a new cycle.

Greg Martin: "My turnaround is inspired by Jimmy Reed and Billy Gibbons. It's versatile: You can use it as a four-bar blues intro or to end a solo." This 12/8 turnaround in *C* begins with the V7 chord at bar 9 of a 12-bar cycle (Ex. 2). The lick occurs over the V7-IV7-I7-V7 change, a blues progression's most harmonically active area. Launch the lick with a muted rake; watch the accents (there are eight of 'em), particularly in bar 2. Slide into the *F* in bar 2 with your second finger. In bar 4, the quarter-bend occurs on the third string only. Fret both *Eb* and *G* with your first finger; gently pull *Eb* away from you while holding *G* still. It's tricky, but sounds great.

Bugs Henderson: "Here's a neat one in *G* that I've used for years in 'Stormy Monday' and other old blues." Some of Ex. 3's highlights:

- *Ab7* is a tritone substitution for *D7*. Thus, the *Am7-Ab7-G7* is a surrogate IIm-V-I (*Am7-D7-G7*).

- A descending chromatic bass line is one of the strongest approaches to a target chord. In this turnaround, the *Bb-A-Ab-G* line leads unequivocally to *G7*, the I.

- To heighten the jazz vibe, use a smoky, round tone and play the sixth-string bass notes legato.

- On beat two, bar 2, percussively whack the *B*, *G*, and *D* strings with your right-hand knuckles.

- At fast tempos, nix *G7*'s hammer-on in bar 2 to keep things relaxed and swinging.

Ex. 1

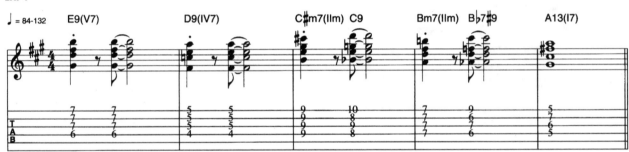

Ex. 2

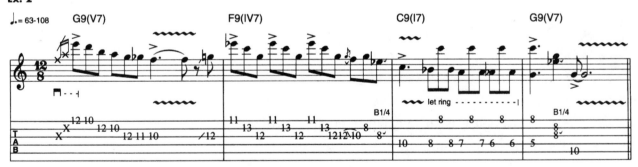

Ex. 3

STEVE VAI
on SOLOING
AS TOLD TO GUITAR PLAYER

Photo: Neil Zlozower

WHEN I SOLO, my realm of thinking is totally derived from the mood, the vamp, the musicians, and the audience—a lot of different factors. I can't get onstage and say I'm going to do *this* every night, because it really doesn't work that way. A song based on an *E* Lydian vamp in 3/4 gives a totally different soloing aura than something like Coltrane's "Giant Steps," which has a chord change every eighth of a second.

Sometimes I develop a solo by taking a story I have in my head and reciting it. And as I say the story, I sing it. No one hears the singing because the amp's too loud. If you play what you're singing, you get sentences. Try it. Listen to what you play—you'll be shocked. It's a totally different approach.

DAVID GRISSOM
ON STEELIN' THE BLUES
AS TOLD TO GUITAR PLAYER

THE FIRST TWO Roy Buchanan records, *Roy Buchanan* and *Second Album*, blew my mind. He would mix total pedal-steel things with slow blues. His tone—an old Telecaster drenched in reverb—was so cool. I spent hours and hours trying to figure out what he was doing.

Here's something to get you headed in this direction. I heard Albert Lee play a similar descending lick. It was so foreign, I tried to figure out what he was doing and wound up with this. You're releasing major or minor seconds into major or minor thirds, as dictated by the scale. As you release each second-string pre-bend against its first-string companion, let both notes sustain against each other. Fret the high note on the *E* string with your first finger. For strength, try bending with a combination of second and third fingers on the *B* string.

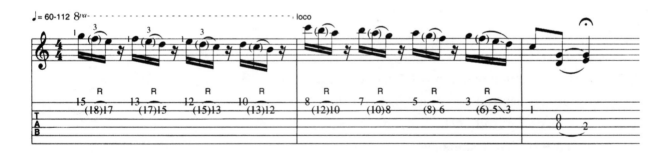

THE FIDDLE SHUFFLE

BY ROGER FERGUSON

YOU KNOW THE ADAGE: Give a man a fish, he'll eat for a day, but teach him how to fish, and he'll eat for a lifetime. This applies to guitar as well. Don't just master a lick, be sure to investigate the concept behind it.

Let's explore a concept that's equally useful in country, bluegrass, Western swing, and blues: When playing over a I-IV7 change, feature the I chord's 3 in your phrase. Keep emphasizing this note across the chord change

as it drops a half-step to become the IV7's ♭7. The result is a hip line that's closely tied to the chord sequence. You can hear this move in the first nine bars of "Sweet Georgia Brown" and in the hook from "Steel Guitar Rag," popularized by Bob Wills and the Texas Playboys.

Let's test-drive this move in a *D-G7* sequence. Ex. 1, a fiddle line, incorporates a shuffle technique used on "Orange Blossom Special" and "Back Up And Push," among others. It's a two-bar, eighth-note pattern that accents every third note while repeating F♯ (*D*'s 3) and then F♮ (*G7*'s ♭7). In Ex. 2, the melody gets a bit more adventurous.

Applied to guitar, this "fiddle shuffle" technique is an example of cross-picking. (Give Doc Watson a listen to hear masterful cross-picking.) You can pick down/down/up, down/down/up, but I recommend strict alternate picking, as it yields a nice bounce and lets your right hand dance for a change.

After hearing *D-G7* played as a I-IV7, you may have to recalibrate your ear for Ex. 3, in which the same progression resolves to a tonic *C*. (To orient yourself, play *C-G7-C*—a I-V7-I cadence in *C*.) Anything goes over the concluding *C* chord; use what's written as a starting point.

In Ex. 4, pick two strings as if they were one. It's tricky playing these double-stops with alternate down and up strokes, but just pretend you're wailing on the world's biggest 12-string.

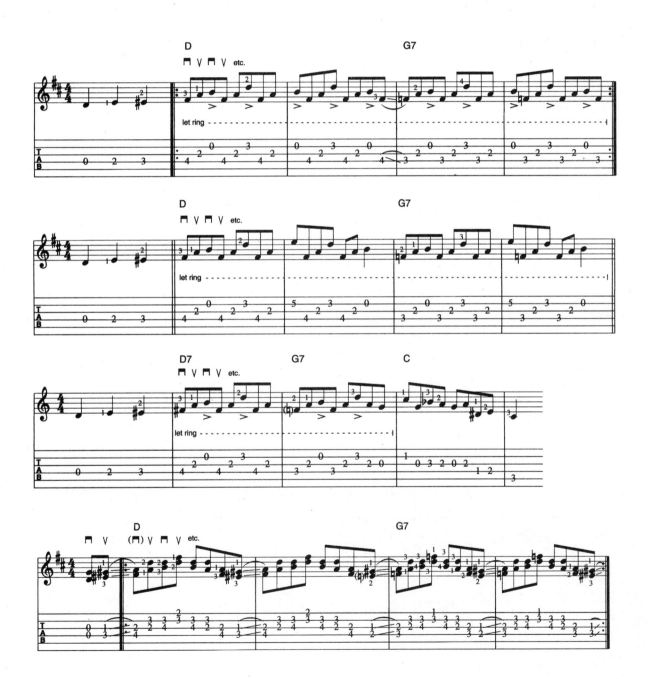

TRITONE TURNAROUND

BY BUGS HENDERSON

HERE'S A USEFUL one-bar turnaround in the key of *A*; it's particularly cool for R&B and uptempo blues. It's easy too—you move one three-note dominant 7th grip in descending half-steps; the action occurs on two string-sets.

There are several ways to analyze this turnaround. The downbeat chords (*A7, F#7, B7, E7, A7*) follow the same root motion as a diatonic I-VIm-IIm-V-I progression in *A*. In this case, however, the chords are all dominant 7s. Another view: *F#7-B7-E7-A7* is a backcycling pattern composed of dominant 7s.

The chords that occur on each upbeat (*G7, C7, F7, Bb7*) follow the root motion of a VIm-IIm-V-I progression in *Bb*; again, we're backcycling in fourths. Each chord in this second group lets you slip into the subsequent downbeat chord from a half-step above: *G7-F#7, C7-B7, F7-E7, Bb7-A7*.

But wait, there's more. Each pair of dominant 7s in beats two, three, and four (*F#7-C7, B7-F7,* and *E7-Bb7*) are tritone twins (see page 33). These chords, whose roots are a diminished fifth apart, share a common tritone and are, therefore, harmonically related.

BARNEY KESSEL'S FOURTH-FINGER WORKOUTS
AS TOLD TO GUITAR PLAYER

PHOTO: JIM CROCKET

MANY PLAYERS AVOID using their fret-hand pinky because it's weak, yet it's weak *because* they avoid it. You can break this cycle by exercising the fourth finger and integrating it into patterns with your other digits.

Examples 1 and 2 build strength and foster independence. Play them at least four times through without stopping, but for no more than three minutes. Use alternate picking and play cleanly. Move the pattern up the neck, gradually increasing playing time and tempo as you gain strength. Eventually, double the tempo and play each exercise as one bar of sixteenth-notes.

Another idea: Try using only the little finger to play a slow ballad's melody. Moving all over the fingerboard with one finger yields a rewarding workout that's both musical and physical.

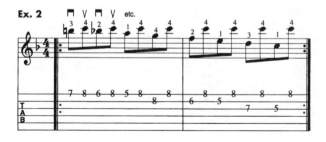

63

MELODY MAGIC

BY BRUCE FORMAN

I PREFER TO THINK of music as language, not math, and focus on sounds instead of formulas. If you listen and keep your thought processes simple, you'll find it much easier to improvise. All the great players I know of started by hearing and repeating melodies, and then creating variations on them. Later, they learned complex theory to open their ears to new possibilities. This is much the way we originally learned to speak.

Learning tunes is of the utmost importance, especially if you expect to play with other musicians. You'll acquire a sense of melody, harmony, and structure. Many inexperienced players don't have the vocabulary to construct melodic phrases over chord progressions, but all players can expressively render a melody and embellish it in a personal way. A song's melody *is* the song.

Let's look at three basic ways to embellish a melodic phrase, such as the opening line to "Autumn Leaves" (Ex. 1). The target tone—our musical destination—is *Eb*. Ex. 2 shows two ways to use appoggiaturas (an ornamentation that precedes a pitch and incorporates notes above and below it) to encircle the target tone; Ex. 3 shows two chromatic approaches to it.

Ex. 1

original phrase

Ex. 2

appogitura (circling the tone)

Ex. 4 uses voice-leading based on harmonic guide tones. In the context of chord changes, guide tones make the resolution. At this point in the melody, the chords are moving from *Cm7* to *F7*—a IIm-V cadence in the key of *B♭*. For our first approach, the melodic motion is *B♭* to *A*—*Cm7*'s ♭7 to *F7*'s 3. This is the most common and strongest voice-leading scheme in IIm-V progressions.

Ex. 4

w/ contrapuntal voice leading

Our second approach features a more colorful, non-diatonic type of chromatic voice-leading. Here, the melodic motion is from *G* to *G♭*—the 5 of *Cm7* to the ♭9 of *F7*. You'd likely resolve this to *F*, the 5 of *B♭*. To experience the harmony from which we extract these two voice-leading approaches, play the

(continued on next page)

Ex. 3

chromatic

progressions in Examples 5 and 6. They illustrate how you can
voice the guide tones on the top of the chords or within them.

Try all these examples up an octave. Internalize the sound
of what you're playing, so you can focus on phrasing and
dynamics. That's what lends true expression to music.

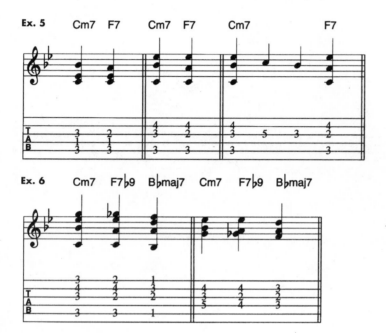

JOHN McLAUGHLIN ON IMPROVISATION AS TOLD TO GUITAR PLAYER

TO REALLY IMPROVISE, to say something you feel at this moment, is the most difficult thing in the world. If you play what you know, then it's not real. To truly improvise requires you not to know anything, in a sense. It's a very difficult and obtuse point. You want to have your knowledge available to you, but the most beautiful thing is to play something for the first time in your life. In this state of mind you see everything before you, every possibility, and you feel you have the ability to move down any avenue you wish— all are suddenly open to you. Music opens the avenues, places you've never been. That can happen in your imagination, but when it occurs in music it's wonderful, because it happens not only inside, but outside at the same moment. It's magic.

AL DiMEOLA'S "MUTOLA" TECHNIQUE
AS TOLD TO GUITAR PLAYER

WHEN I FIRST started taking guitar lessons, I was very self-conscious around my parents and relatives. I never wanted to have people say, "What's that noise?" In those days, electric guitar was not accepted like it is today, so I started muting the strings with my right hand to reduce the volume. Years later, I would mute the strings as a musical effect, but only then did I realize that it had become a part of my style. I generally use the lower part of the palm (Photos 1 and 2).

Tonal payoffs. I like the way the notes pop out when you mute them. They project more, and it makes what you're playing very defined, especially on the low notes.

With this technique, I don't mute every note, and I apply different muting pressures to different notes. If I want one note to ring out more than another, I'll lessen the pressure. Sometimes it can be light enough that it doesn't sound like muting but simply cleans up the sound. It's important to mute just right, so that it doesn't end up sounding too thumpy.

Muting tricks. When muting, I'll pick normally, although if I want a note to be a little brighter, I'll add some fingernail to an upstroke (Photo 3). I'll mute lightly, and while picking upward, the string will first touch the pick, then my first fingertip, and finally the fingernail. I also have this thing where I can get a phasing sound. Although it's very difficult and subtle, I've been using it a little now and then. It is very similar to the upstroke I described, but involves releasing and reapplying the muting pressure during the picking strokes.

Another way to approach the "Mutola" is to simultaneously strike the string with both your pick and index fingertip. This works well on downstrokes and upstrokes. You can create many different textures by muting. All it takes is practice.

Photo 1

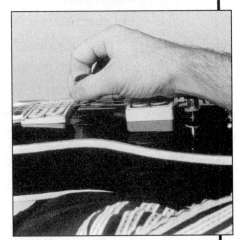

Photo 2

Photo 3   PHOTOS: LEN DELESSIO

HIP TURNAROUNDS

BY BUGS HENDERSON, RONNIE EARL & GREG MARTIN

WE ASKED **THREE** *of our favorite players—the red-hot Bugs Henderson, blues ace Ronnie Earl, and tone-ful Greg Martin of the Kentucky Headhunters—to share some of their hippest, most useful turnarounds. —AE*

Bugs Henderson: "I love turnarounds because they add an element of surprise to a familiar blues or a standard. You can create a little shock thing, especially if you use cool, strange chords. By the time the last change lays down, tension is high and you've got everyone's attention. It feels great when you release that tension and resolve to the familiar progression."

Prepare for Bugs' turnaround by playing the four chords in Ex. 1a. You're in the key of *C*. Right-hand fingers, pick, or a combination of the two work equally well. Check out the top common tone and the stepwise motion on the *G* string.

In the turnaround proper (Ex. 1b), the chords are staggered; lead into each one from its lowest note. Observe the *let ring* indications and, as you slide into *C9*, don't forget to hit the fifth-string root. Substitute *Bb9* (Ex. 1c) for *G7sus4* to create a nifty chromatically descending line in the lowest voice (*Bb-A-Ab-G*). "Play turnarounds loud and fast," advises Bugs, "and they'll always fit."

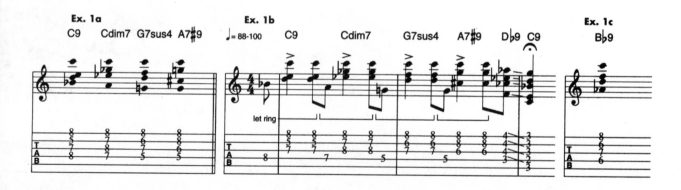

Ronnie Earl: "Mine's a classic blues turnaround in *E*. It's versatile and fun to play. I usually fret the first three chords using 2nd, 1st, and 3rd left-hand fingers, low to high, but experiment with other grips that include the pinky. If you're using a flatpick, carefully mute the fifth string with whichever finger you're fretting the sixth string with."

First get acquainted with the moves in Ex. 2a. Like our previous turnaround, this one seesaws the chords, with the low note leading into each form (Ex. 2b). Again, watch the *let ring* indications. This turnaround is highly mobile. Transposed to *A*, Ex. 2c boasts an alternate triplet rhythm and a new twist at the end. Ain't nothing but common tones and stepwise motion happening here.

Ex. 2a

Ex. 2b

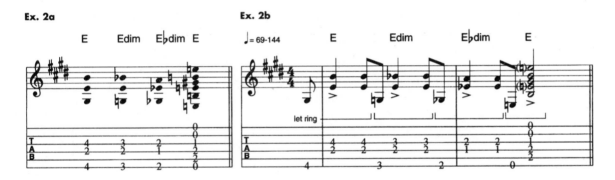

Ex. 2c

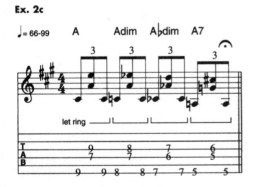

(continued on next page)

Greg Martin: "My turnaround is in the spirit of Lightnin' Hopkins. I play it fingerstyle, although a mixed pick-and-finger approach works too. The passage covers the V7-IV7-I7 move of an *E* blues."

Execute Ex. 3 with a warm, burnished tone, and give the last fretted *E* a real good wiggle. For an added bit of funk, scoop into the bass notes in bars 1 and 2 with your fretting hand thumb.

Ex. 3

ERIC JOHNSON
on SPEED PICKING
AS TOLD TO GUITAR PLAYER

AS YOU'RE PICKING down, pick at an angle so you go diagonally from the guitar body's left horn down to the control knobs. On the way back up, do the opposite diagonal. This way, you don't hit the strings dead-on, therefore minimizing the amount of extra noise and friction. If you were to look at someone doing that real fast, it would be a circular technique— you're skimming over the string. As you pick diagonally, also pick from the guitar body up into the air, up and down, perpendicular to the string. You have to bounce your wrist. It's hard, and it almost works against playing fast sometimes, but that bounce gives you all the tone of the fretted note without all the extraneous noise. I hold the pick with my thumb and first finger and don't use the pointy end as much as the pick's side to brush the note.

PHOTO: MAX CRACE

7 3

CONTRIBUTORS

A jazz studies professor at the University of North Texas, **FRED HAMILTON** directs the school's guitar ensemble. He is also an instructor at the Jamey Aebersold Summer Jazz Workshops and an active clinician. Savor his velvet touch on *Looking Back on Tomorrow* (Wolf Tales, 1823 Sharon Dr., Corinth, TX 76205).

DAVID HAMBURGER teaches at the National Guitar Workshop. For his solo album, *King of the Brooklyn Delta,* or info on clinics and private instruction, write to Chester Records, Box 170504, Brooklyn, NY 11217. Hamburger's *Electric Slide Guitar* is available from Hal Leonard.

BRAD CARLTON is living proof that not all monster players live in New York, Nashville, or L.A. Based in St. Petersburg, Florida, Carlton has been teaching for 20 years and prides himself on his versatility. His rep in the region is that he can play anything.

To appreciate twangmonster **JIM CAMPILONGO,** listen to his moody *Table for One,* which you can find at most Tower Records stores, or order from Cdnow.com or World Records (1-800-742-6663). Email Jim at jc@bluehenrecords.com.

DREW BEARSE is a longtime *Guitar Player* reader from Portland, Oregon.

GREG MARTIN plays lead guitar with the Kentucky Headhunters, loves Jesus, vintage guitars, blues, and barbecue. After releasing *Pickin' on Nashville* in 1989, Martin and his bandmates received the ACM award for Top New Vocal Group. In 1990, the album won a Grammy and a CMA award, both for Album of the Year. Martin is currently working on a solo gospel/blues project.

DAVE RUBIN has played with Chuck Berry, Screamin' Jay Hawkins and James Brown's JBs. His Hal Leonard instructional book/CD packages *Inside the Blues 1942-1983, Art of the Shuffle,* and *Power Trio Blues* are full of historical photos, background info and hip licks.

A clinician and product specialist for Aria guitars, **JOE DALTON** leads his own band and has performed with Arlen Roth and Johnny Rodriguez. Dalton's Hot Licks video *Country Jazz* is full of fret-melting moves.

STEVE TROVATO is an associate professor at the University of Southern California and a staff instructor at Hollywood's Musician's Institute, where he has taught for 14 years. An expert in roots rock, blues, and country, he has performed with Albert Lee, Albert Collins, Robben Ford, Scott Henderson, Jerry Donahue, and Paul Gilbert. Trovato has authored several country guitar books and has a country-rock instructional video on REH.

MIKE HICKEY has played with Cronos, Carcass, Cathedral, and Venom. He supplements his speed/death/thrash grind fetishes with doses of Mahavishnu and Holdsworth.

Odd-meter specialist **TIM SPARKS** is the 1993 National Fingerpicking Champion. His *Guitar Bazaar* features intense fingerstyle compositions influenced by Middle Eastern and Balkan music. You can see Sparks perform his music on a companion video (both CD and video are distributed by Acoustic Music, 1610 Crestview Ave., Seal Beach, CA 90740). View his web page at members.aol.com/picksparks, and send e-mail him at Tcguitar@aol.com.

CHARLES CHAPMAN is a professor Boston's Berklee College of Music, where he has taught guitar since 1972. His CD *In Black & White,* a jazz duet with bassist Rich Appleman, is available from Box 251, Littleton, MA 01460.

Head picker at Hollywood's GIT, **KEITH WYATT** has authored books on harmony, theory, ear training, and blues, and helped develop the schools guitar curriculum. He has also directed instructional videos by Albert Collins, Marty Friedman, Paul Gilbert, and Al Di Meola. Check out his own fine REH *Rockin' the Blues* video.

Known for his unusual chord voicings and pensive, probing lines, **JOHN STOWELL** is one of the Pacific Northwest's premier jazz guitarists. Experience Stowell's sensuous sound on *Lines & Spaces* (GSPJAZ, 514 Bryant St., San Francisco, CA 94107).

As evidenced by the Hot Licks video *Mastering Lead Guitar,* **MICHAEL LEE FIRKINS** is known for his canny vibrato bar techniques.

Ricky Skaggs, Kathy Mattea, Emmylou Harris, and Marty Stuart are among those who have put **RAY FLACKE**'s snappy licks to good use. His excellent Homespun video *Country Telecaster Virtuosity* covers a world of tasty Tele tricks. For info on Rays solo work, clinics and private instruction, write to Box 120776, Nashville, TN 37212.

Acclaimed for his lean, impassioned playing, **RONNIE EARL** paid dues in Roomful of Blues and has performed with B.B. King, Eric Clapton, Stevie Ray Vaughan, Buddy Guy, Otis Rush, Albert Collins and Muddy Waters. Recommended: Earl's Rounder CD, *Language Of The Soul,* and Hot Licks video *Blues Guitar With Soul.*

Check out resophonic wizard **BOB BROZMAN**'s Homespun videos *Learn to Play Bottleneck Blues Guitar, Traditional Hawaiian Guitar,* and the two-volume *Hot Guitar.*

FRANK GAMBALE is a two-time winner of the *Guitar Player* Readers Poll, and a Grammy Award winning guitarist. He heads the guitar department at the Los Angeles Music Academy and wrote the curriculum for the school's one-year guitar program. Visit Frank's website at www.FrankGambale.com or write him at Box 1248 Hollywood, CA 90078.

Master picker **BUGS HENDERSON** knows American electric guitar inside and out. For a tightwire trip into surf, rockabilly, blues, swamp boogie, and twangy rock, hear his *Daredevils of the Red Guitar.*

Joe Ely, John Mellencamp, James McMurtry, and Toni Price have all turned to Austin's **DAVID GRISSOM** for his fretboard magic. His band Storyville plays a compelling blend of soul and rock—just listen to *Dog Years* [Code Blue/Atlantic].

ROGER FERGUSON has played and recorded with Mark O'Connor and Jerry Douglas. Wielding flat-top, fiddle, and mandolin, Roger gigs steadily throughout the Pacific Northwest in Double Stop, a duo with wife Lynne.

The burning **BRUCE FOREMAN** draws accolades wherever he plays. Barney Kessel calls him "one of the great lights," and the late Leonard Feather labeled Bruce "a composer of rare merit." Check out Foreman's *The Jazz Guitarists Handbook, Jazz Guitar Soloing* video, and *Forman on The Job* CD on Kamei. All three are available from GSP, 514 Bryant St., San Francisco, CA 94107.

The late **VIC TRIGGER** was a frequent contributor to Miller Freeman Publications.

ANDY ELLIS is *Guitar Player* magazine's Lessons Editor.

Touring with Deep Purple, **STEVE MORSE** created a new audience for his refined technique and eclectic solos. Morse's fingers fly in *Structural Damage* (High Street/Windham Hill).

Chet Atkins, Ted Greene, Steve Masakowski, Brent Mason, Danny Gatton and Philip deGruy are among the many pickers who cite the late **LENNY BREAU** as a major influence. His harp harmonics and simultaneous lead/comping technique revolutionized finger-style jazz.

An admitted blues and swing junkie, **DUKE ROBILLARD** loves to confound fans with his rich and eclectic approach. *Duke Robillard Plays Jazz: The Rounder Years* is packed with jump blues and swing guitar.

East Coast bop-rocker **MIKE STERN** first gained exposure working with Miles Davis. Stern's tough, fast, and lean improvisations continue to wow listeners. Hear Stern's many moods on *Standards (And Other Songs)* on Atlantic.

One of Americas jazz guitar greats, **BARNEY KESSEL** is a living link to Charlie Christian.